SPORTS Bloopers

SPORTS
Bloopers
ALL-STAR FLUBS AND FUMBLES

Mark Huebner

and

Brad Wilson

FIREFLY BOOKS

A FIREFLY BOOK

Published by Firefly Books Ltd. 2003

First printing

Publisher Cataloging-in-Publication Data (U.S.)
(Library of Congress Standards)

Huebner, Mark.
  Sports bloopers : all-star flubs and fumbles / Mark Huebner , Brad Wilson. —1st ed.
[128] p. : col. photos. ;   cm.
Summary: A collection of 150 photographs that highlight embarrassing moments in professional and amateur sports.
ISBN 1-55297-627-0 (pbk.)
1. Sports — History. 2. Sports — Miscellanea. I. Wilson, Brad.
II. Title.
796/.097 21   GV576.H84 2003

National Library of Canada Cataloguing in Publication Data

Huebner, Mark, 1958-
  Sports bloopers : all-star flubs and fumbles / Mark Huebner, Brad Wilson.

ISBN 1-55297-627-0
  1. Sports--Miscellanea.   I. Wilson, Brad, 1966- II. Title.
GV707.H82 2003   796   C2003-902808-9

Published in the United States in 2003 by
Firefly Books (U.S.) Inc.
P.O. Box 1338, Ellicott Station
Buffalo, New York 14205

Published in Canada in 2003 by
Firefly Books Ltd.
3680 Victoria Park Avenue
Toronto, Ontario, M2H 3K1

Design and layout: Tinge Design Studio

Printed in Canada

The Publisher acknowledges the financial support of the Government of Canada through the Book Publishing Industry Development Program for its publishing activities.

INTRODUCTION

Gym class. There you stand among your classmates. Baggy shorts letting in a cold breeze. Your t-shirt flaps like a smelly flag around your unbuff upper body. The gym teacher is blowing her whistle and dividing you all up into teams. It doesn't really matter what the game is. You already know the outcome. The few natural athletes in your class will dominate the action and the scoring. The rest of you will be dragged along like gulls following the wake of battle cruisers.

The one thing that breaks the monotony of running back and forth across a wet field or stuffy gymnasium is enjoying the spectacle of someone else making a fool of himself. Usually it's one of us. Or us. But on those rare occasions when it's an actual athlete who screws up, it's … it's … it's repressed. Barely a smirk. Hardly a giggle. Is it because we respect their ability, talent and physical prowess? Hardly. It's because no one wants to get an atomic wedgie later in the change room.

It is at *this exact moment* you develop your appreciation for sports bloopers. And this book allows you to safely enjoy those times when athletes are caught with their pants down. Often literally, as you'll discover.

That said, we've found this book is best enjoyed when you change into your old gym clothes and pound back a big bag of potato chips.

A big impression.
Atlanta Braves' Andruw Jones
runs out of running room chasing
a home run.

Safe!

Chicago Cubs' catcher slides into the White Sox dugout.

Heads, you lose.

Kim In-Sub (blue) and Yurity Meinichenko wrestle
at the 2000 Olympic Games.

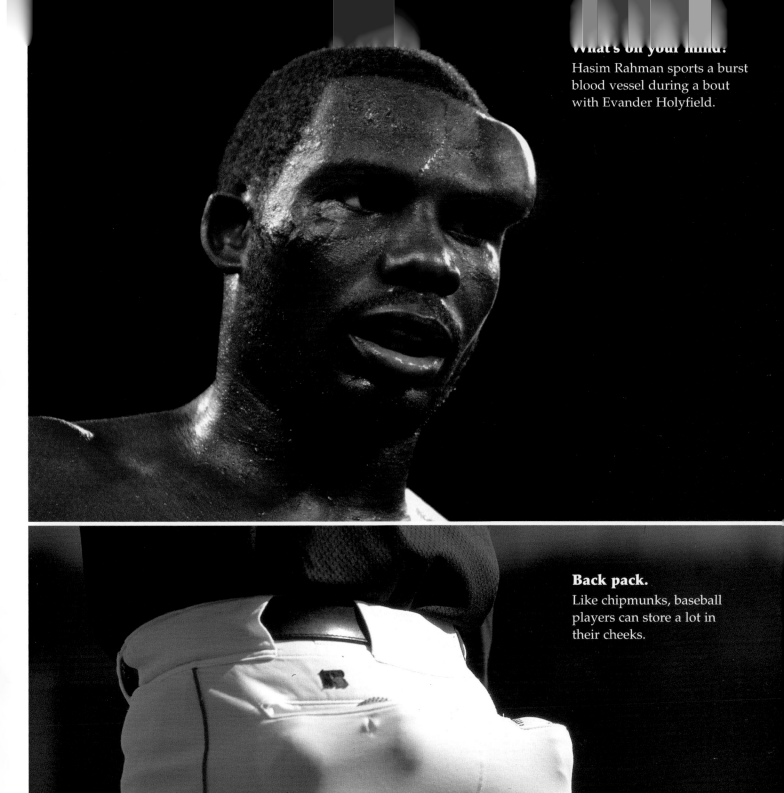

What's on your mind?
Hasim Rahman sports a burst blood vessel during a bout with Evander Holyfield.

Back pack.
Like chipmunks, baseball players can store a lot in their cheeks.

Heels over head.

Abigael Bakker tumbles over
Little Sparkle during a European
championship.

UFO: Unmounted Flying Object.
Shay Barry bails during Grand National
steeplechase.

Up and over Downunder.

Daniel Hall at the Crusty World Tour
in Australia.

A deadly game of chicken.
The San Diego Chicken flips a Florida
Marlins player.

**Pro scouting report: Needs to grow
another foot.**

Wide receiver Anthony Chambers of the
Purdue Boilermakers.

**Next, they'll clean out the locker ▶
room with a flame-thrower.**

A helicopter flies over a cricket field
to dry it after heavy rains.

Getting the game off the ground.

Dallas Stars' Aaron Garvey collides with
a New Jersey Devil.

Backseat diver.
San Diego Padres catcher Carlos Hernandez piles on John Rocker as he slides home to score.

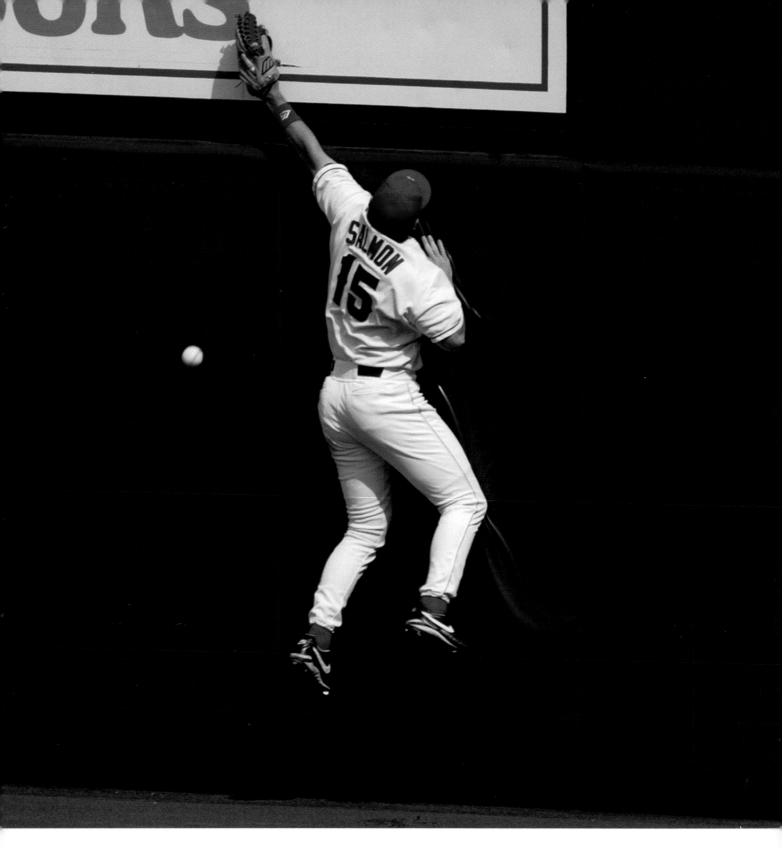

Salmon up the creek.

Anaheim Angels' Tim Salmon.

One giant leap.

A soccer player reaches for the moon.

Flying off the handlebar.
Hector Barbera crashes in front of Gabor Ralmacsi and Andrea Ballerini at the British 125cc Grand Prix.

Flat out effort.
John McEnroe at an exhibition game
against Boris Becker at the 2002 US Open.

◄ **Winner by a nose.**
Jean Gatien serves at an Olympic
table tennis match in Sydney.

Bottoms up.

Li Hongli fails to lift 197.5 kg at the
Asian Games in Korea.

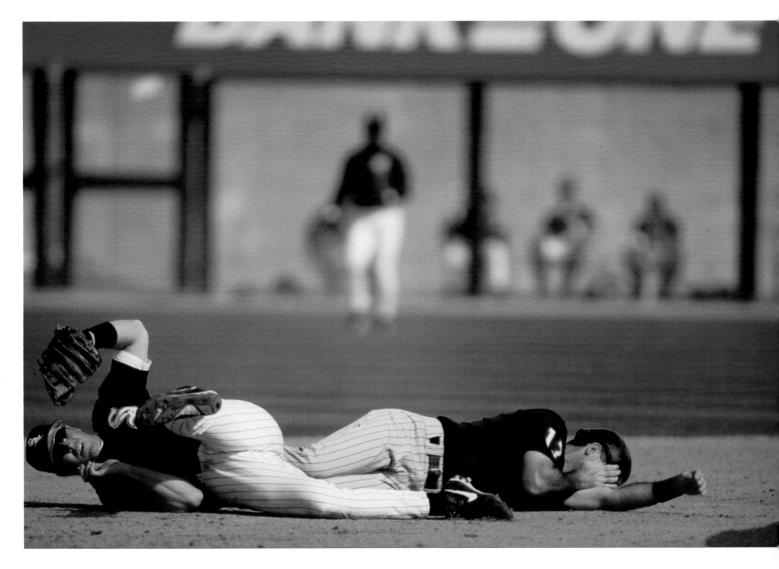

In need of a seventh inning stretcher.
Chris Snopek and Steve Scarsone collide at a
spring training game.

Follow threw.

Tiger Woods reacts to a bad shot
during the final round of the Target
World Challenge.

And you think *your* game stinks.
Nick Faldo retrieves his ball during the
Nissan Open.

Aussie rules football.

The Geelong Cats mix it up with the
Sydney Swans.

Aussie rules basketball.

Melbourne Tigers try to hang on to the ball
during a game against the Victoria Titans.

◄ The bottom dropped out.
Mark Mercuri of the Essendon Bombers.

Strip maul.
Filippo Inzaghi is mobbed by joyous
soccer fans.

Getting the bum's rush.
Canberra Raiders' Anthony Colella
in an Aussie football game against
the Sydney Sharks.

America's cups. ▶

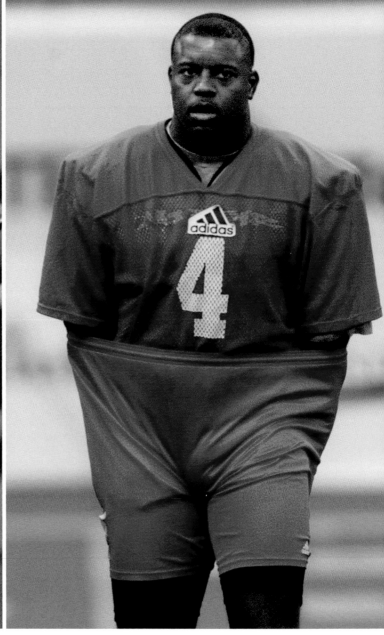

Do-it-yourself wedgie.

Argentine soccer star Martin Palermo
misses his second penalty kick.

Tight end.

Football player Darryl Hall of the
Calgary Stampeders adjusts his, um,
shorts during practice.

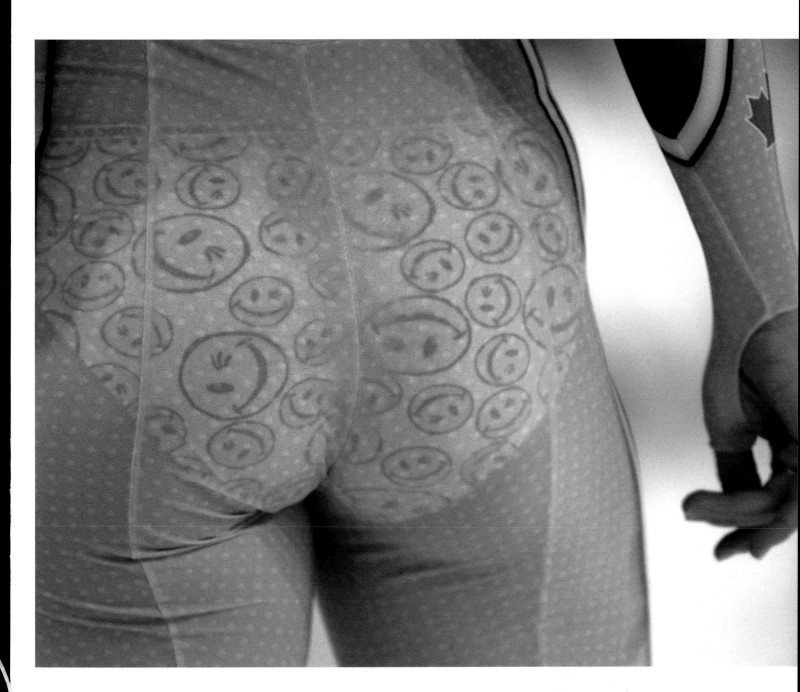

Smile.
Canadian speed skater Krisy Meyers makes the most of her transparent racing suit.

Please.

Call.

Doctor.
Marc Montoya rides the rail at the
2002 Yahoo! Sports Big Air and Style
Jib Jam in Park City, Utah.

Poke check.

Fingertip control.

One on one.

Two on one.

Playing from behind.

Riddick joins the Sopranos.

Andrew Golota belts Riddick Bowe.

In over his head.
Marco Barrera (right) defeats Erik
Morales at the World Featherweight
Championship.

Ball in glove.

New York Yankees' Derek Jeter tags
out Anaheim Angels' David Eckstein.

Chin up.
Salomon Olembe (right) and Daoyda
Diakité at the African Nations Cup.

A ref landing.

Rob Shick flops during the Stanley Cup
playoffs.

Cliff hanger.
Florida Marlins' Cliff Floyd tries to catch
a foul ball.

Up the creek without a clue.

◀ **The new sign for "steal second."**

Wave good-bye.

A boat crew capsizes at the Australian Surf
Life Saving Championships.

Leash laws strictly enforced.
Rob Machado wipes out at the 2002 Xbox
Pipeline Masters Hawaii.

Off track.

Two-man Japanese bobsleigh crashes at the 1988 Winter Olympics in Calgary.

◄ **On sail now.**

Robby Naish midway through a loop at the 1999 Windsurfing World Cup.

Go for a spin.
Dan Wheldon walked away
from this crash at the Indy 500.

◀ **One way to beat traffic.**
David Coulthard's Williams Renault is hoisted clear
of the track after crashing with Jean Alesi's Ferrari.

Model citizen.
A model demonstrates a new cover-up tube designed to be thrown over streakers.

◀ **Hat in hand.**
A streaker is discreetly led away by police during a British rugby match in 1974.

Run for cover.

Ball handler.

Why streaking never caught on at hockey games.

This streaker fell to the rink from the top of glass. Paramedics were called to help clear the ice.

Razing the bar.

The snore of the crowd.

Spectators contain their enthusiasm
at the Henley Rowing Regatta.

Tall in the saddle. ▶

A spectator watches the action during
the PGA Grand Slam in Kauai, Hawaii.

Lose by a hair.
Beijing police detain a basketball fan
after the crowd reacted to a no-show
by Kobe Bryant.

A rowdy fan gets carried away. ▶
During a security simulation, a
Colombian riot policeman slides
down a rope with a fan.

Will the real Anna Kournikova please stand up.

Thank you.

A bad hangover.

A fan hangs out during a game between the
Atlanta Braves and the New York Mets.

Wet Sox.
Two-time All-Star Chicago White Sox outfielder Al Smith gets a free beer during the 1959 World Series.

Attempted cover-up.
Argentine players protect themselves against a free kick.

◄ **Sign of the times.**
An Arizona Diamondbacks' fan teases the New York Yankees during the World Series.

Ricky Clemons

Peter Nowak

THE ALL-STAR HALL OF PAIN.

Luis Figo

Kobe Bryant

Padraig Harrington

Jarrod Moseley

THE ALL-STAR HALL OF PAIN.

Chris Clarke

Sergio Garcia

Feat in the air.

The men's 150m sprint at the
World Junior Championships.

Something always happens after making the last car payment.

Christian Fittipaldi recovers from a collision at the Indy Carnival in Australia.

Fall into line.

Katsuo Nakatake topples during a
sprint race at the 1984 Los Angeles
Olympics.

Professional cyclists occasionally make a pile.

Riders recover after a crash during the 2002 *Tour de France*.

Stuff it.

Weapons of glass destruction. ▶

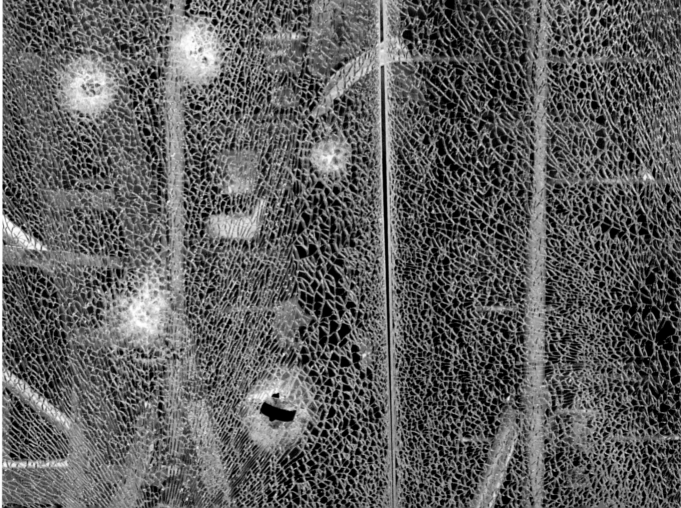

Actually, this hurts less than playing for the Cubs.
Sammy Sosa's batting helmet stops a Salomon Torres fastball.

Breakaway. ▶
Ottawa Senators' Chris Phillips.

Touchdown!

Toronto Maple Leafs' Darcy Tucker hurdles
New York Islander goalie Chris Osgood.

Up next: spectator jumping!
Stuart Tinney and horse Tex plow through the crowd at the Badminton Horse Trials.

Rein of terror.

◄ **Jockey for position.**

Boongoggle.

◀ **Ride every mountain.**

Bringing up the rear.
Kris Draper collides with Toni Lydman
during the World Senior Ice Hockey
Championship.

Make a wish and pull. ▶
This Anaheim Mighty Duck
runs afoul.

Looking for a real fight.
WWE wrestler Chris Jericho at the NHL
All-Star Celebrity Game.

◀ **Hat trick.**
Movie director and goaltender Bobby Farrelly
at the NHL All-Star Celebrity Game.

Roadside assistance.
Medical attention during
the *Tour de France*.

◄ **Trying to pull off a win.**

Palm Puppy.
St. Petersburg, Florida.

Show me the tummy. ▶
Suomo wrestler Konishiki
is tested.

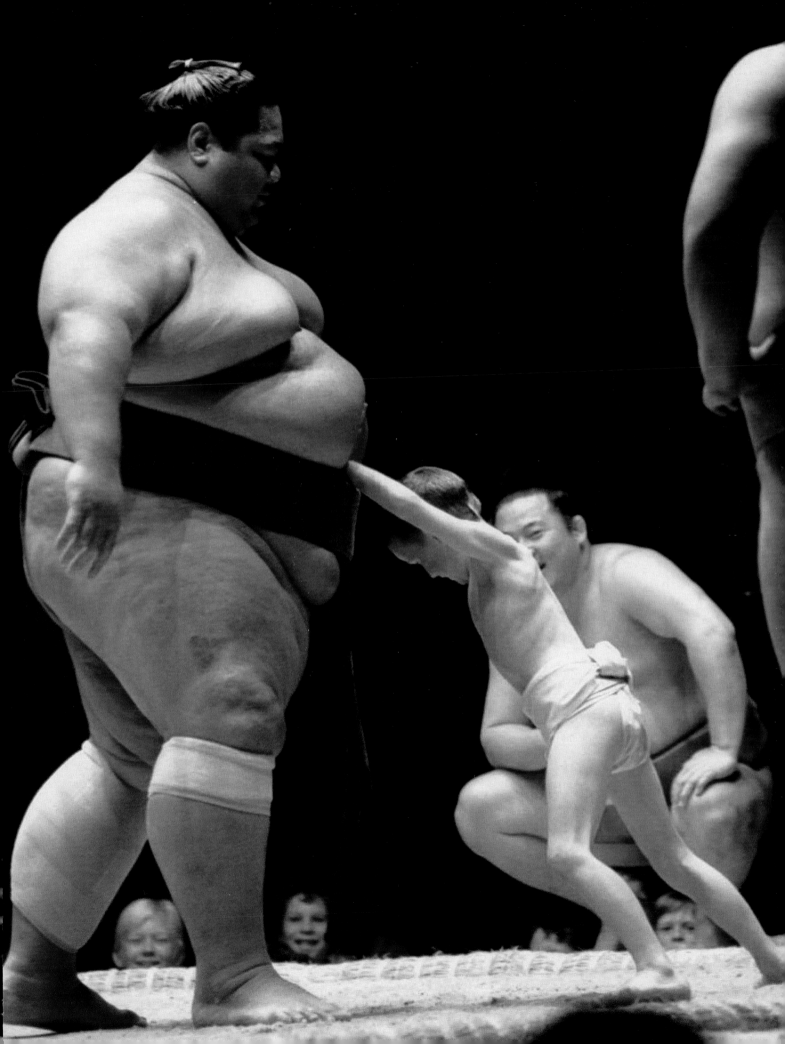

Don't lose your head.

Wrestlers compete for bronze at
the 2002 Commonwealth Games.

Best seat in the house.
Tunisia's Khaled Badra lands on Japan's
Shinji Ono during the 2002 World Cup.

... aaand *stay* out!
Dodgers' Kirk Gibson stumbles past
second base and St. Louis Cardinals'
Luis Alicea in 1989.

Check please.

Dean McAmmond avoids a body check by
Ingemar Gruber during the World Senior
Hockey Championship.

Facing stiff opposition.

After the wedgie, they gave
him a purple nurple.

Rugby tip #1: If the ball doesn't come loose, try the head.

Sami Rabaka tackles Guy Easterby during a rugby international match.

Take that.
Anaheim Angels' David Eckstein and Baltimore Orioles' Chris Singleton in double play action.

Double play.

Puppy love.
A dog frolics on the clay court
during the 2003 French Open.

Birdie brain.
A committed fan looks on during the
Doral Ryder Open.

Arms agreement.

Keeping a stiff upper arm.
British cricket players react to a dropped
catch during a match against Australia.

Flying buttress.

Incredibull.

Crowned.

Hasim Rahman in the fourth round
of his bout with Lennox Lewis.

Eye sticking. ▶

Dave Andreychuk's elbow catches Mike
Foligno's eye.

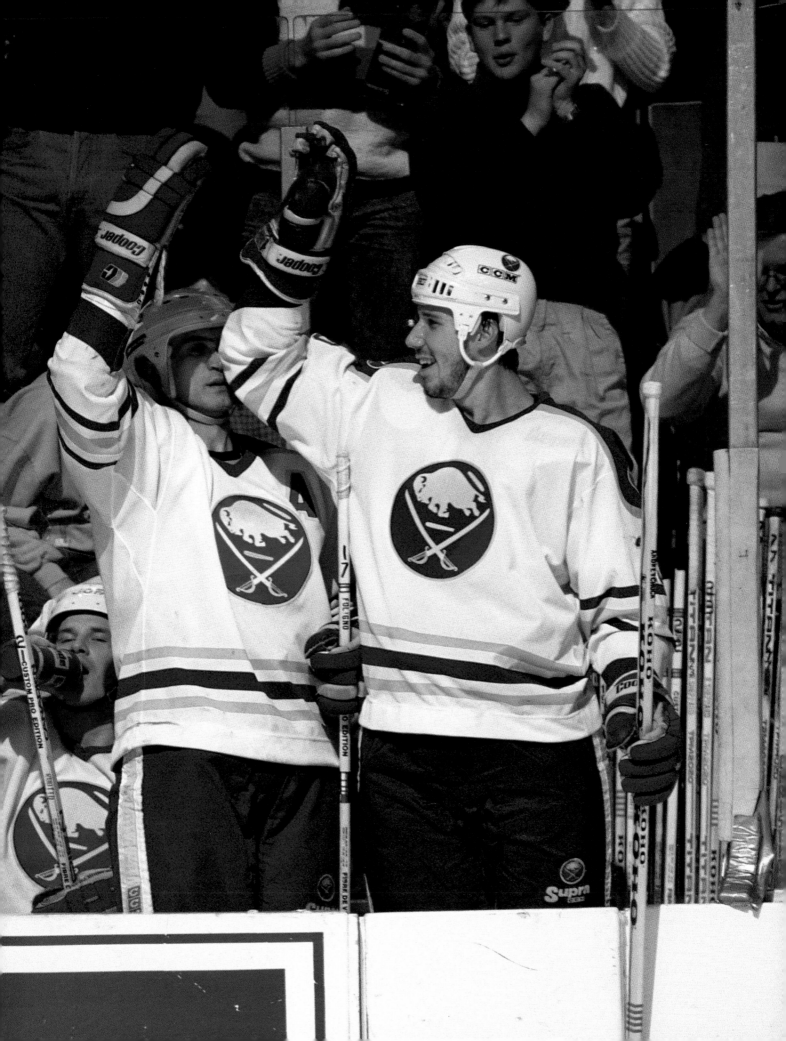

He forgot only one thing ...

... **gravity.**

A promising career cut short.

Stuntman Ed Gaedel was signed by the St. Louis
Browns to pinch-hit against the Detroit Tigers.
He was walked four times with Jim Delsing
being sent in to run for him. Gaedel's contract
was legal, but the rules were soon changed.

Short putt. Long memory.

In 1970, Doug Sanders missed this short putt on the 18th to lose his chance of winning The Open at St. Andrews, Scotland. Twenty-five years later he said, "Do I ever think about it? Hell, I've been known to go as long as five minutes without thinking about it."

Hull or high water.
Flipped boat at the Australian Jetsprint
Boat Championship.

◄ **Crash course.**
The Polish team crashes during the 4-man
bobsleigh event at the 1928 Winter Olympic
Games in St. Moritz, Switzerland.

**The ol' pushed-over-the-kneeling-kid
routine.**

A Team USA player collides with a German
player during the 1992 Winter Olympics.

Speed trap.

Kristin Krone of the USA slides into the
safety nets at the 1992 Winter Olympics.

Flash
photography.

PHOTO CREDITS

p.72　Al Bello/Getty Images

p.73　Charles Knoblauch/AP

p.74　Colin Braley/Reuters

p.75　Ruben Sprich/Reuters

p.76 (top left)　Elsa/Getty Images

p.76 (top right)　Jonathan Daniel/Getty Images

p.76 (bottom left)　Shaun Botterill/Getty Images

p.76 (bottom right)　Lisa Blumenfeld/Getty Images

p.77 (top left)　Andrew Redington

p.77 (top right)　Chris McGrath/Getty Images

p.77 (bottom left)　Ian Walton/Getty Images

p.77 (bottom right)　Andrew Redington/Getty Images

p.78　Nicolas Gohier/Agence Vandystadt

p.79　Pascal Rondeau/Getty Images

p.80　David Cannon/Getty Images

p.81　Bruno Fablet/Reuters

p.82　A. Pichette/Bruce Bennett Studios

p.83 (top)　Brian Winkler/Bruce Bennett Studios

p.83 (bottom)　Brian Bahr/Getty Images

p.84　AP Photo

p.85　Agence France Presse

p.86　Dave Sandford/Getty Images

p.87　Phil Cole/Getty Images

p.88　Darren England/Getty Images

p.89　Adam Pretty/Getty Images

p.90　Agence-Vandystadt-Agence de Presse Photographique Vandystadt/Allsport France

p.91　Nicolas Gouhier/Agence Vandystadt

p.92　Anatoly Maltsev-STF/Agence France Presse

p.93　L.Redkoles/Bruce Bennett Studios

p.94, 95　Donald Miralle/Getty Images

p.96　Agence-Vandystadt-Agence de Presse Photographique Vandystadt/Allsport France

p.97　Gérard Vandystadt/Agence Vandystadt

p.98　Chris Livingston/Getty Images

p.99　Australia Melbourne Reuters News Picture Service

p.100　Scott Barbour/Getty Images

p.101　Pedro Ugarte-STF/Agence France Presse

p.102　Mike Powell/Getty Images

p.103　Yuri Kadobnov/Agence France Presse

p.104　Robert Cianflone/Getty Images

p.105　Shaun Botterill/Getty Images

p.106　Jamie McDonald/Getty Images

p.107　Jeff Gross/Getty Images

p.108　Jeff Gross/Getty Images

p.109　Jamie Squire//Getty Images

p.110　Christophe Guibbard/Agence Vandystadt

p.111　Harry How/Getty Images

p.112　Jeff Haynes-STF/Agence France Presse

p.113　Nick Wilson/Getty Images

p.114　Agence-Vandystadt-Agence de Presse Photographique Vandystadt/Allsport France

p.115　Bruno Bade/Agence-Vandystadt/Allsport France

p.116　Mike Franco/Reuters

p.117　Dan Hamilton

p.118,119　Getty Images

p.120　AP Photo

p.121　Hulton Getty/Getty Images

p.122　I.O.C./Getty Images

p.123　Darren England/Getty Images

p.124　Rick Stewart/Getty Images

p.125　Getty Images

p.126　Bruno Bade/Agence Vandystadt

PHOTO RESEARCH

Jim Codrington
Mark Huebner
Lionel Koffler
Brad Wilson
Michael Worek

SPECIAL THANKS TO:

Jim Codrington; Brian and Christine at Tinge Design Studio; Dan Liebman; Howie Burke, Joe Fava and Jason Sundberg at Getty Images; Lizabeth Menzies and Susan Williams at Agence France Presse; Alain at Agence Vandystadt; Bruce, Gary and Lisa at Bruce Bennett Studios; Anne-Marie Beaton at CP Images; and Fatima Dias at Reuters.